Nine Minutes
on Monday

☐ MODEL

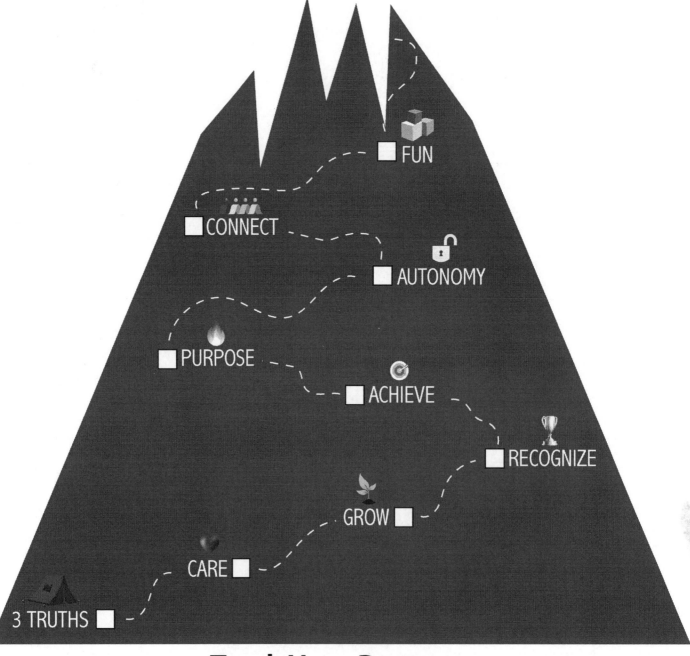

☐ FUN

☐ CONNECT

☐ AUTONOMY

☐ PURPOSE

☐ ACHIEVE

☐ RECOGNIZE

☐ GROW

☐ CARE

3 TRUTHS ☐

Track Your Progress

Nine Minutes on Monday
The Quick and Easy Way to Go from Manager to Leader

Three Truths about Leadership

1. You are paid to _____.

   - So focus your energy helping your people be
     as_____as you need them to be.

2. Leadership is the_____

   - So lead with passion and excellence.

 The Principle of Weighted Relationships

3. Leadership is a_____.

   - So you can get better with_____.

> **The Numbers**
> 50% of work satisfaction is determined by relationship with immediate boss.
> *Saratoga Institute*
>
> Exit interviews from 20,000 people revealed the supervisor's behavior was the main reason why they quit.
> *Saratoga Institute*
>
> Relationship with a manager largely determines an employee's length of stay.
> *Gallup Organization*

70% The amount managers account for in the variance of Employee Engagement scores across business units. - Gallup

Motivation and Engagement

Motivation and engagement are complex concepts with many variables. Motivation is the psychological feature which arouses an organism to action toward a desired goal.

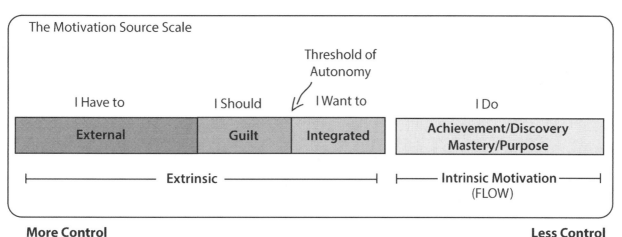

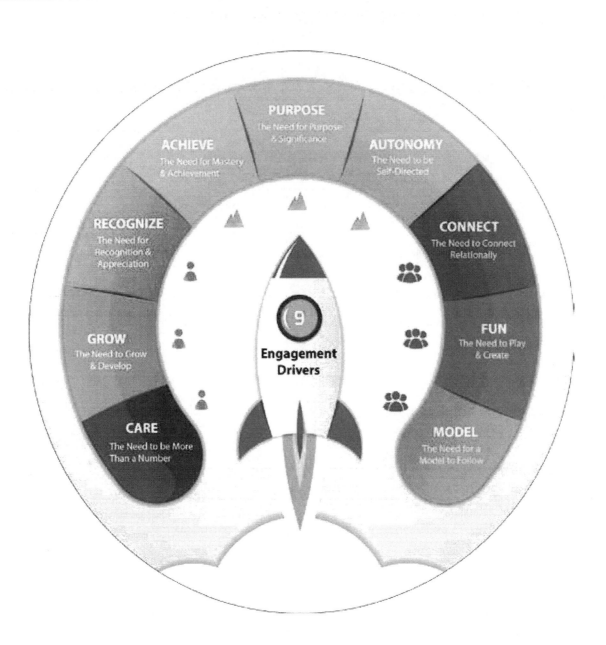

The nine needs are like switches, which ignite purpose, passion and engagement.

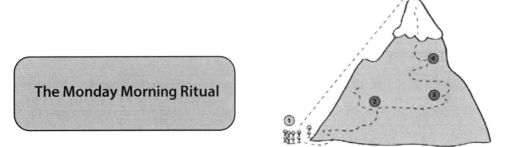

The Monday Morning Ritual

The Power of a Fixed Line

THE THREE TRUTHS WORKSHEET

Use this worksheet to with the module titled The Three Truths.

List the names of at least three people in leadership positions that had a major impact on elevating your performance. These could include coaches, mentors, or bosses.

Under each name write three things they did to have such an impact on you.

1. _____
_____
_____

2. _____
_____
_____

3. _____
_____
_____

1. _____
_____
_____

2. _____
_____
_____

3. _____
_____
_____

1. _____
_____
_____

2. _____
_____
_____

3. _____
_____
_____

What similarities, if any, did you notice about these people who had a significant impact on your performance?

Think of a time where you were firing on all cylinders. What was going on? In other words, describe the situation you were in that elicited a peak performance from yourself.

What insights does this situation give you about performing at your best?

Part I
The Employee

Care - The Need to be More than a Number.

An employee's need to be valued as an individual is one of the top engagement drivers world-wide. Reward, recognition, and a manager's genuine interest is essential to an employee's engagement.

Reasons to Care

1. Caring is directly linked to_____.

2. Caring improves_____ .

3. Caring helps you become a better_____ .

4. Caring is the_____ thing to do.

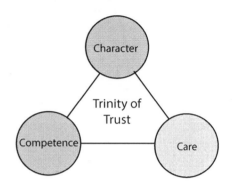

Trinity of Trust

Character

Competence

Care

Trust built on this side

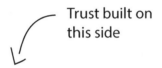

Wants what is best for me

Wants something from me

Practical Ways to Care

1. Showing_____ Interest

   • Vital Statistics

   • The Walk-a-bout

2. The Corporate_____ .

3. Lift a_____ .

Minute 1

How will you take a genuine interest in your employees this week?

The Need to be More than a Number

When employees feel that their workplace cares for them as people, it increases their engagement by strengthening bonds of trust. This exercise will help you evaluate how well you know your employees as individuals and provide a starting point for you to take a genuine interest in them as people.

Using the table below, fill in the names of your direct reports and what you currently know about their Vital Statistics. Then use simple tools like the walkabout to take a genuine interest in their lives and show that you as a manager care.

Employee	Family	Hobbies/Interests	Career Goals	Corporate Bday

Grow - The Need for Growth and Progress

Studies show that one of the highest drivers of engagement is when employees feel they have a chance to grow and develop. (Towers/Perrin 2008)

How to Help Someone Grow

1. Growth Begins with_____ .

   Clarifying Question: What will help them to be more_____?

   *Break their role down into_____ and establish a _____.

2. Choose a_____.

   - The power of On-the-fly Coaching

   - When training use the 3 P's
     - Purpose

     - Principle

     - Practical

3. Help them see their_____ .

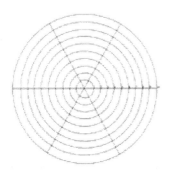

Coaching Wheel

*Visual assessments are great feedback tools.

The key is getting your employees to_____their development

Turn your employees into_____.

GROWTH & DEVELOPMENT WORKSHEET PLANNER

For each of your direct reports try to identify three areas of growth that would make them more effective. They could be knowledge gained, a skill learned, or something in their behavior changed.

Name	Growth Area 1	Growth Area 2	Growth Area 3
	Ideas/Tools	Ideas/Tools	Ideas/Tools

Name	Growth Area 1	Growth Area 2	Growth Area 3
	Ideas/Tools	Ideas/Tools	Ideas/Tools

Name	Growth Area 1	Growth Area 2	Growth Area 3
	Ideas/Tools	Ideas/Tools	Ideas/Tools

Name	Growth Area 1	Growth Area 2	Growth Area 3
	Ideas/Tools	Ideas/Tools	Ideas/Tools

Recognize - The Need to be Valued

Recognition is feedback and helps meet our basic need for _____.

⭐ Recognition is one of the easiest and cheapest ways to motivate others and yet it is often a neglected art. Why do you think?

Recognition has multiple benefits. It...

1. Acts as a _____.

2. Shapes _____.

3. Builds Trust and _____.

4. Provides _____.

Keys to Reward and Recognition

1. _____.

2. Use _____ language.

3. _____.

4. Connect it to a _____.

57%
Prefer praise from direct manager.

21%
Prefer praise from higher up.

The Midas Touch

Here are three things you can recognize at any given time.

Achievement or Progress	Behavior	Quality
Any accomplishment is a prime place for recognition as well as forward progress toward a goal.	Look for behaviors that support the culture you are trying to build.	Look for qualities in them which you or your organization value.

The Recognition Codes

People connect what they do with who they are. Remember the 'Refrigerator Picture?' When you value your employees for who they are and what they produce you reinforce effective behavior, as well as motivate, strengthen relational bonds, and link their efforts to the larger picture.

Below are the Recognition Codes. Use them as a template to create a recognition statement for one of your direct reports this week.

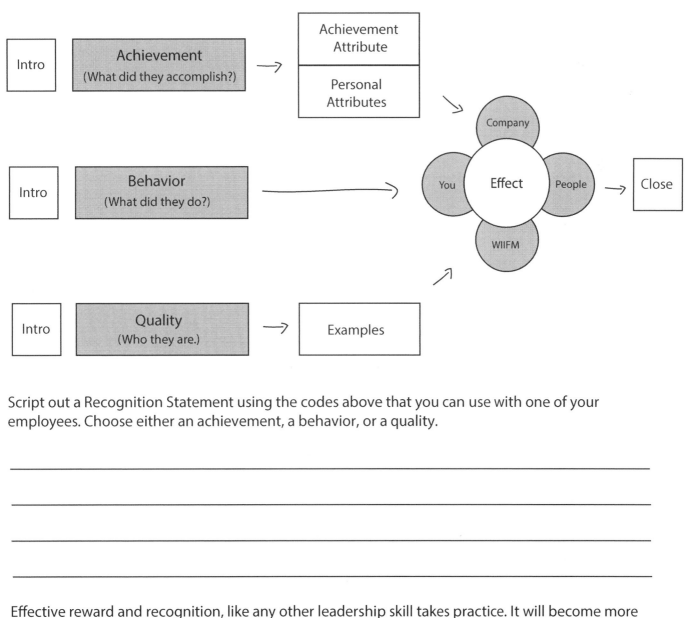

Script out a Recognition Statement using the codes above that you can use with one of your employees. Choose either an achievement, a behavior, or a quality.

_____

_____

_____

_____

Effective reward and recognition, like any other leadership skill takes practice. It will become more natural over time. Take your Recognition Statement and deliver it to one of your employees this week.

THE REINFORCEMENT STRATEGY WORKSHEET

Fill out this page to help you identify the areas where you can use recognition and appreciation to drive results, shape behavior, create culture and encourage your staff.

List your Company Values
List the values of your organization below. If you do not presently have a formal list then write out the values you have for your team.

_____

_____

_____

_____

_____

Behaviors that Demonstrate These Values
Beside each value write at least two staff behaviors that would demonstrate the value being lived out at work.

_____

_____

_____

_____

_____

_____

_____

_____

_____

Key Behaviors
List the Behaviors and Actions most important to your team's success.

_____   _____

_____   _____

_____   _____

_____   _____

_____   _____

Recognition Codes

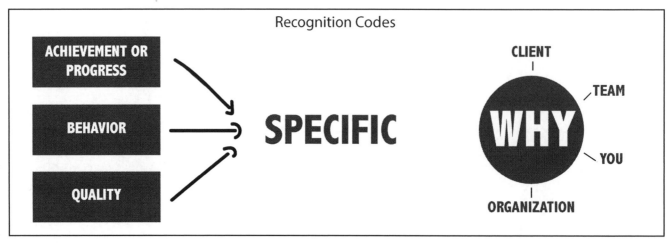

Part II
The Job

Achievement- The Need to Make Progress Toward a Goal.

Humans are a forward moving species who find purpose and meaning in accomplishments and progress. When the workplace helps nourish an employee's need to achieve, the job itself becomes the source of motivation.

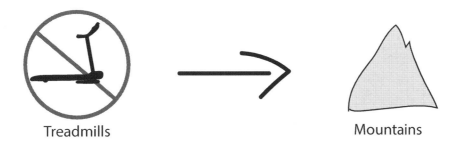

Treadmills → Mountains

FLOW States

A state of complete absorbtion and engagement where time passes quickly and one loses themself in a task. (Mihály Csíkszentmihályi)

Conditions of FLOW

1. Clear _____ or _____.

   Employees need to know the goal they are pursuing or at very least what success looks like.

   Employees need goals that are_____
   and _____.

Motivation is in the GAP

2. Balance between **Skill** and _____.

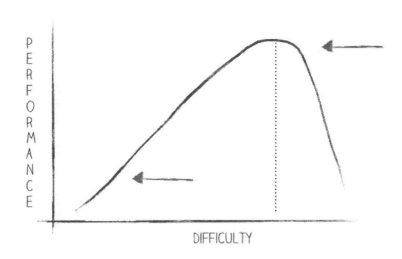

PERFORMANCE

DIFFICULTY

FACT:
One of the most replicable findings in all psychological literature is that Challenging and Specific goals lead to an increase in performance.

Mastery - The Need to Achieve

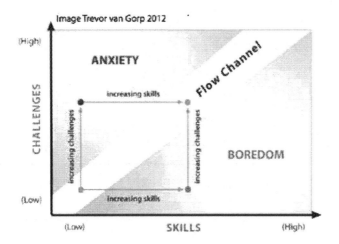

Employees enjoy a boost in engagement when they are pursuing challenging but reachable goals.

This sweet spot is where they enter into a FLOW State.

3. Consistent _____.

If we can't give an employee feedback on their progess they are probably on a treadmill. We want to move them onto a mountain.

The Feeback Loop

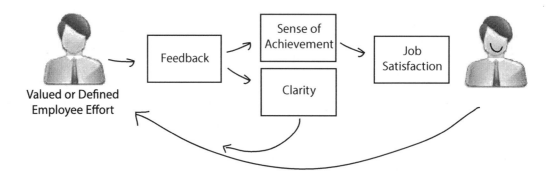

An employee's progress is going to come in one of three basic forms.

1. They are ahead of where they should be. Try_____

2. They are right where they should be. Try_____

3. They are behind and need to do better. Try_____

18

MOUNTAINS & MASTERY

Everyone needs a mountain to climb. Specific and challenging goals are proven to elevate performance. Use the worksheet below to think through each of your direct reports to make sure you are maximizing their engagement through their need for Achievement.

Employee Name	They know what's expected of them.	They have a measurable goal to pursue.	The goal challenges them.	There are short-term milestones.	There is a way to track their progress.	You give them feedback.	Next Steps
	☐	☐	☐	☐	☐	☐	
	☐	☐	☐	☐	☐	☐	
	☐	☐	☐	☐	☐	☐	
	☐	☐	☐	☐	☐	☐	
	☐	☐	☐	☐	☐	☐	
	☐	☐	☐	☐	☐	☐	
	☐	☐	☐	☐	☐	☐	
	☐	☐	☐	☐	☐	☐	
	☐	☐	☐	☐	☐	☐	
	☐	☐	☐	☐	☐	☐	

"Everybody has their own Mount Everest they were put on this earth to climb."
~ Seth Godin

Purpose - The Need for Significance and Contribution
One of the most powerful motivators in the world is purpose. Employees want their lives to matter and contribute to something larger than themselves. Workplaces that help employees connect purpose to pay, will have an engaged, productive, and motivated culture.

The Second Paycheck
Purpose helps tap into that deep seated desire that our lives _____.

Four questions to help connect purpose to pay.

1. Who do you_____?

2. What_____has your product, or service been_____?

3. How do you make a_____here?

"A sense of purpose is the fuel that drives people to invest their whole selves."

— James Robbins

4. What is your _____?

One of the most powerful ways to link purpose to pay is through_____.

Can you think of a recent story that would help connect purpose to pay?

FROM PURPOSE TO PAYCHECK WORKSHEET

Linking purpose to paycheck is a powerful source of motivation. Try to answer the questions below to find things you can use to remind your employees of the larger role they play .

Who do we serve?

Who is your customer? Brainstorm a list of all your customers both internal and external.

What job is our product or service hired to do?

Brainstorm the tangible reasons why people purchase your services and/or products. Think benefits.

What is your vision for your team or department?

How compelling is your vision for where you want to lead your group or department? Try to clarify your vision here and then plan on communicating it to your staff.

There's power in a story.

Can you think of a story of how your product or service made a difference in a customer or client's life? If so, write it here and then tell it to your staff to remind them of the larger part they play.

Freedom - The Need for Autonomy

When employees perceive they have some degree of control over their lives and work they are happier, more creative, persist longer and enjoy greater overall well-being.

☆ All around the world, people hate having a_____boss because they infringe on our need for_____.

5 Benefits of Autonomy

1. Creates _____.

2. Inspires greater _____.

3. Boosts creativity.

4. Employees will_____ longer.

5. Better at_____.

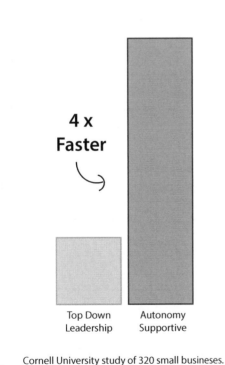

Growth Rate

4 x Faster

Top Down Leadership

Autonomy Supportive

Cornell University study of 320 small businesses.

Simple Ways to Promote Autonomy

1. Give_____when possible.

2. Seek their _____.

3. Let them have authority.

4. Tap into their_____.

5. Make someone an area _____.

6. Remove a _____.

7. Make it safe to _____.

☆ Autonomy must be balanced with_____. This creates security.

THE AUTONOMY DRIVERS WORKSHEET

Fill out this page to help you identify areas where you can help each of your emplyees experience more autonomy in their role so they ultimately take more ownership.

Autonomy Drivers

Select at least one Autonomy Driver for each employee and then use this tool as a reference each week.

Employee Name	Give Choice or Flexibility	Involve them in a Brainstorm	Seek their Input	Make them an Area Expert	Remove a Restriction	Give them Authority	Defer a Decision to them	Partner on Solving a Problem	Let them Set a Goal
	☐	☐	☐	☐	☐	☐	☐	☐	☐
	☐	☐	☐	☐	☐	☐	☐	☐	☐
	☐	☐	☐	☐	☐	☐	☐	☐	☐
	☐	☐	☐	☐	☐	☐	☐	☐	☐
	☐	☐	☐	☐	☐	☐	☐	☐	☐
	☐	☐	☐	☐	☐	☐	☐	☐	☐
	☐	☐	☐	☐	☐	☐	☐	☐	☐
	☐	☐	☐	☐	☐	☐	☐	☐	☐
	☐	☐	☐	☐	☐	☐	☐	☐	☐
	☐	☐	☐	☐	☐	☐	☐	☐	☐
	☐	☐	☐	☐	☐	☐	☐	☐	☐
	☐	☐	☐	☐	☐	☐	☐	☐	☐

Part III
The Environment

Connect - The Need for a Functional Team

An employee's psychological need for connection is foundational to satisfaction in the workplace. A dysfunctional team will erode morale, and hinder productivity. Team building is an ongoing process that requires attention and focus.

Three Components of Healthy & Effective Teams:

1. Healthy teams have Psychological _____.

"In a team with high psychological safety, teammates feel safe to take risks and feel confident that no one on the team will embarrass or punish them for admitting a mistake, asking a question, offering a new idea." - re:Work with Google - Project Aristotle

Fostering Safety
The following ideas will help you create more Psychological Safety & Trust among your team.

Protecting Safety
A great leader is always on the lookout for behaviors that threaten the Psychological Safety of the team. These include things such as:

* As a leader you have no choice but to lean in and address these unhealthy behaviors.

2. Team members are _____.

In order to foster dependability, team members must be willing to be _____, this includes the _____.

3. There is Clarity and Structure.

Members need to have clear RPG's.

R_____.

P_____.

G_____.

WORKING AS A TEAM EXERCISE

Choose one of the exercises below to do with you and your team.

☐ Exercise #1 - Protecting the Team

Think through your team and identify if there are any of the following unhealthy behaviors present. For each one you identify make a commitment to address the issue so that it does not continue to hurt team morale.

Problem Behavior	The plan to deal with it including when.
☐ Unresolved conflict	_____
☐ Bully	_____
☐ Unhealthy rivalry	_____
☐ Slacker	_____
☐ Pessimist	_____
☐ Disrespectful	_____
☐ Victim or Drama King/Queen	_____
☐ Never accepting criticism	_____
☐ Rude	_____
☐ Gossip/backbiting	_____
☐ Critical of others	_____
☐ Disrespctful body language	_____
☐ Not keeping commitments	_____

☐ Exercise #2 - Create a Code of Conduct

Have a discussion with your team about Team Norms and see if you can agree on an operating Code of Conduct for working together. Below is a sentence starter you can use to get the conversation rolling. See if you can come up with no more than 7-10 rules that will govern how your team behaves.

"If we were to create our own code of conduct that would shape how we operate as a team what would we want it to say. Please try to keep all answers positive instead of negative. i.e. Instead of saying "Do not send any ALL CAPS emails." say, "Send only respectful courteous emails." Our goal is to come up with 7-10 guidelines to help us grow as a team."

Play - The Need for Fun

All work and no play makes Jack a dull boy. The research is in. When employees have fun at work they are more productive, less stressed, and more creative.

Here are five ways that fun can improve productivity in your workplace:

1. Fun is the ultimate_____buster.

2. Fun boosts_____.

3. Fun strengthens relational bonds.

4. Fun improves _____.

5. Fun starts with _____.

> **Fear:**
> Fun at work means no work
> is getting done.
>
> **Fact:**
> Workplaces that have fun are generally more productive and healthier than ones that are short on fun.

 Brainstorm Moment
What are some ways you can have appropriate fun at work?

Ideas

- Appoint someone as the D.O.F. (Director of Fun)

- Find ways to inject humor into your team meetings.

- Plan an event where the team can get out and have some fun together.

-

-

Eliminating Fun Suckers from the Environment

Inefficiencies, red tape, and minor frustrations can compromise the enjoyment of the work environment.

Identify Fun Suckers and commit to_____% improvements as a team.

THE 1% IMPROVEMENT PLANNER

In each box identify an area in your team, department, or organization that needs to be improved, is a frustration, an inefficiency, or is no fun. Then see if you can list a few 1% improvements you could make to begin improving this area.

Fun Suckers, and Inefficiencies   1% Improvements

☐ _____
☐ _____
☐ _____
☐ _____
☐ _____
☐ _____

Fun Suckers, and Inefficiencies   1% Improvements

☐ _____
☐ _____
☐ _____
☐ _____
☐ _____
☐ _____

Fun Suckers, and Inefficiencies   1% Improvements

☐ _____
☐ _____
☐ _____
☐ _____
☐ _____
☐ _____

Take a moment at your weekly or monthly meeting to continually achieve 1% improvements until the problem is solved. Then find a new problem, frustration or fun sucker and work on it.

Model - The Need to Have an Inspiring Example to Follow

Employees desire to work for an inspirational and competent manager. When managers continually lead by example and model traits known to be inspirational, employees respond with increased trust, excitement, and buy-in.

Great Leaders are:

1. _____.

    Knowing who _____.

    Knowing what you_____.

2. _____.

    Leaders are not content with the_____.

3. _____.

Leaders give people the _____to act.

4. _____.

    a. The power of _____Authority

    b. The Leadership Virtues
       - Acting with _____.

       - Interpersonal _____.

       - Courage

       - Strength or _____.

> **Tip**
> Modelling the values of your organization makes sense and creates alignment as well as encourages others to do the same.

What motivates you?	**Leading Up**
	It's important to communicate with your boss what they can do to help you perform _____.

THE LEADERSHIP COMPASS

Gaining clarity on the type of leader you aspire to be.

Read through the list of leadership characteristics and circle the 5 items that you MOST want to model as a leader and then write them in the space below..

- ☐ Respectful
- ☐ Authentic
- ☐ Fairness
- ☐ Inspirational
- ☐ Visionary
- ☐ Results Driven
- ☐ Humility
- ☐ Hard Working

- ☐ Knowledgable
- ☐ Servant Leader
- ☐ Courageous
- ☐ Integrity
- ☐ Resilient
- ☐ Confidence
- ☐ Humor
- ☐ Principled

- ☐ Accountable
- ☐ Risk Taker
- ☐ Optimistic
- ☐ Focused
- ☐ Loyal
- ☐ Passionate
- ☐ Likeable
- ☐ Charismatic
- Other _____

My Top 5 Leadership Values

Write out the list of your top 5 leadership values below.

_____

_____

_____

_____

_____

Leadership Values to Grow in:

Pick 3 leadership characteristics from the above list that are not currently strengths but you see the need to grow in.

_____

_____

_____

Intentional Leadership

As a leader what do you want to be known for? Write a simple sentence or two describing the leader you aspire to be.

THE PURSUIT OF LEADERSHIP MASTERY
WORKSHEET PLANNER
How to engage in the art of Deliberate Practice.

Identify no more than three Leadership Skills or Domains you would most like to grow in. For each one write a list of micro skills and/or behaviors that make up that domain. These micro skills will provide you short actionable tasks you can practice each week so that your leadership skill increases. For example, if you chose giving Performance Feedback as one of your domains, then it is made up of multiple micro skills you can work on such as, establishing safety and rapport, body language, mastering objections, how to start the conversation, and follow up conversations. Each of these becomes a separate skill that you can work on each week to improve.

☐ Enforcing Standards	☐ Time Management	☐ Decisiveness
☐ Coaching	☐ Self Confidence	☐ Open Minded
☐ Communicating Strategic Vision	☐ Intentional Example	☐ Decision Making
☐ Performance Feedback	☐ Relationship Building	☐ Proactive not Reactive
☐ Dealing with Difficult Behavior	☐ Listening	☐ Manage Setbacks
☐ Holding Others Accountable	☐ Ability to Confront Others	☐ Challenging the Proces
☐ Being More Fun	☐ Empowering Others	☐ Passion
☐ Having More Executive Presence	☐ Setting Realistic Goals for Staff	☐ High Energy
☐ Exerting More Emotional Control	☐ Negotiation	☐ Building Team
☐ Leading Change	☐ Ability to Inspire	☐ Problem Solving
☐ Presentation Skills	☐ Engaging and Motivating Staff	☐ Delegating
☐ Leading Effective Meetings	☐ Rewarding Others	☐ Priority Management

List as many micro skills for this below.	List as many micro skills for this below.	List as many micro skills for this below.

Each week select a couple of micro skills from the list above and set goals to improve. Make sure these goals are specific and challenging. Then, seek feedback either by reviewing your performance or by enlisting a coach or mentor to help.

9 Nine Minutes on Monday Template

Minutes on Monday

Use this blank template to help create your leadership goals for the week. Hold yourself accountable at the end of the week by striving to complete all of your goals.

Minute 1 **Care**	When and with whom will you show genuine interest or concern? *Walkabout Monday morning around 10:30am*	Completed ✓
Minute 2 **Grow**	Who will you help grow and develop this week? *Give feedback to Cory on how she does with running the meeting this week as well as pointers for improvements for next time.*	Completed ✓
Minute 3 **Recognize**	This week who will you reward or recognize? And how will you do it? *Talk to Kelly after staff meeting about the effect her ideas had on the team yesterday. She helped unlock people's rigid thinking.*	Completed ✓
Minute 4 **Mastery**	This week who will you give feedback to? *Talk to Jane about her progress on her project.*	Completed ✓
Minute 5 **Purpose**	How will you connect purpose to pay for an employee or the team this week? *Share with the team the newspaper clipping about the family lost at sea because of a faulty motor.*	Completed ✓
Minute 6 **Autonomy**	How can you support or promote someone's autonomy this week? *Ask Cory to design a better system for workflow communications.*	Completed ✓
Minute 7 **Connect**	What small thing can you do this week to increase team stickiness? *Have Josh tell us about his trip to Nepal for a couple of minutes at staff meeting tomorrow.*	Completed ☐
Minute 8 **Play**	Where is one place you can inject fun into the job or team this week? *This place is always fun...*	Completed ☐
Minute 9 **Model**	What leadership quality will you model this week? *Positive attitude despite the challenges the company is facing.*	Completed ✓

Nine Minutes on Monday 8-Week Tracker

Use this form to help keep track of your distribution of leadership priorities for each employee and your team. At the end of 8 weeks look for any patterns or inconsistencies.

Employees Names →

Priority	Instruction	Kelly	Cory	Bubba	Mary	Jane
Care	Place a check mark each time you meet this need for each employee over the next 8 weeks.	✓✓		✓	✓	
Grow	Place a check mark each time you meet this need for each employee over the next 8 weeks.					
Recognize	Place a check mark each time you meet this need for each employee over the next 8 weeks.	✓			✓✓✓	
Mastery	Place a check mark each time you meet this need for each employee over the next 8 weeks.		✓		✓	
Purpose	Place a check mark each time you meet this need for each employee over the next 8 weeks.					
Autonomy	Place a check mark each time you meet this need for each employee over the next 8 weeks.				✓✓	

After 5 Weeks

Team Needs	Instruction	Week 1	Week 2	Week 3	Week 4	Week 5	Week 6	Week 7	Week 8
Connect	Place a check mark each time you do something to promote or protect team.	✓	✓			✓			
Play	Place a check mark each time you do something to have fun as a team.		✓			✓			
Model	Place a check mark for each week that you're clear on what leadership quality or behavior you are modelling.	✓	✓	✓	✓✓	✓			

Nine Minutes on Monday 8-Week Tracker

9 Minutes on Monday

Use this form to help keep track of your distribution of leadership priorities for each employee and your team. At the end of 8 weeks look for any patterns or inconsistencies.

Employees Names ——→

Employee Needs

Care	Place a check mark each time you meet this need for each employee over the next 8 weeks.
Grow	Place a check mark each time you meet this need for each employee over the next 8 weeks.
Recognize	Place a check mark each time you meet this need for each employee over the next 8 weeks.
Mastery	Place a check mark each time you meet this need for each employee over the next 8 weeks.
Purpose	Place a check mark each time you meet this need for each employee over the next 8 weeks.
Autonomy	Place a check mark each time you meet this need for each employee over the next 8 weeks.

Team Needs

Team Needs	Instruction	Week 1	Week 2	Week 3	Week 4	Week 5	Week 6	Week 7	Week 8
Connect	Place a check mark each time you do something to promote or protect team.								
Play	Place a check mark each time you do something to have fun as a team.								
Model	Place a check mark for each week that you're clear on what leadership quality or behavior you are modelling.								

35

Nine Minutes on Monday Template

Use this blank template to help create your leadership goals for the week. Hold yourself accountable at the end of the week by striving to complete all of your goals.

Minute 1 — Care
When and with whom will you show genuine interest or concern?
Completed ☐

Minute 2 — Grow
Who will you help grow and develop this week?
Completed ☐

Minute 3 — Recognize
This week who will you reward or recognize? And how will you do it?
Completed ☐

The Employee

Minute 4 — Achieve
This week who will you give feedback to?
Completed ☐

Minute 5 — Purpose
How will you connect purpose to pay for an employee or the team this week?
Completed ☐

Minute 6 — Autonomy
How can you support or promote someone's autonomy this week?
Completed ☐

The Job

Minute 7 — Connect
What small thing can you do this week to increase team cohesion?
Completed ☐

Minute 8 — Fun
Where is one place you can inject fun into the job or team this week?
Completed ☐

Minute 9 — Model
What leadership quality will you model this week?
Completed ☐

The Environment

NINE MINUTES WEEKLY IDEA TOOLKIT

Here are some of the ideas you have learned over this course to help you in your Monday Morning Ritual to motivate and engage your staff. Each week try to pick just one from each category to put into practice with an employee. If none of these ideas resonate, add your own.

The Need to be More than a Number

- [ ] Schedule a Walkabout.
- [ ] Learn something you didn't know about an employee.
- [ ] Lift a Load.
- [ ] Acknowledge a Corporate Birthday.
- [ ] Share a personal story.
- [ ] Let someone teach you about their hobby.
- [ ]

The Need to Grow

- [ ] Get clarity on an area of growth for an employee.
- [ ] Have a coaching time with an employee.
- [ ] Teach something you learned recently.
- [ ] Challenge an employee to take it higher.
- [ ] Give someone feedback on their growth.
- [ ] Express your belief in an employee.
- [ ]

The Need to be Recognized

- [ ] Recognize a company value.
- [ ] Reinforce a Key Behavior.
- [ ] Use Gossip Recognition.
- [ ] Recognize up.
- [ ] Recognize someone's effort or progress.
- [ ] Appreciate a character quality.
- [ ]

The Need for Achievement

- [ ] Scan for employees stuck on treadmills.
- [ ] Help someone set a goal or milestone.
- [ ] Make adjustments to the difficulty of someone's goal.
- [ ] Check in with employee on progress.
- [ ] Give performance feedback on progress.
- [ ] Confirm that an employee knows exactly what's expected. Define success.
- [ ]

The Need for Significance

- [ ] Connect their job to something bigger.
- [ ] Share a story of the impact your organization has had on a customer.
- [ ] Help someone see their impact on the team.
- [ ] Remind an employee of your vision.
- [ ] Ask someone what they care about at work?
- [ ] Remind them of who you serve.
- [ ]

The Need for Autonomy

- [ ] Ask an employee for advice.
- [ ] Pull someone in to solve a problem.
- [ ] Remove a restriction, approval needed or red tape.
- [ ] Appoint someone an area expert.
- [ ] Let an employee make a final decision.
- [ ] Give someone choice or flexibility.
- [ ] .

The Need to Connect

- [ ] Scan team for any problem behavior.
- [ ] Get everyone to contribute at meeting.
- [ ] Get two employees to work together.
- [ ] Resolve a conflict among employees.
- [ ] Ask someone to take a new hire for lunch.
- [ ] Get team to share good news at meeting
- [ ]

The Need for Fun

- [ ] Search online for ideas on having fun at work and pick one that's appropriate.
- [ ] Hold a contest.
- [ ] Plan for something fun at a meeting.
- [ ] Schedule an informal event for team.
- [ ] Bring treats to a meeting.
- [ ] Identify a Fun Sucker and commit to 1% improvement.
- [ ]

The Need for a Model to Follow

- [ ] Review your Leader Mission Statement.
- [ ] Pick one skill to practice and improve.
- [ ] Pick a Quality or Value to model.
- [ ] Model accountability and ask team for feedback as a leader.
- [ ] Remind your team about your vision for where you are heading.
- [ ] Review personal leadership gaps from last week and make adjustments.
- [ ]

www.jamesrobbins.com

Copyright 2018 The James Robbins Company LLC

Nine Minutes on Monday Template

Use this blank template to help create your leadership goals for the week. Hold yourself accountable at the end of the week by striving to complete all of your goals.

Minute 1 — Care
When and with whom will you show genuine interest or concern?
Completed ☐

Minute 2 — Grow
Who will you help grow and develop this week?
Completed ☐

Minute 3 — Recognize
This week who will you reward or recognize? And how will you do it?
Completed ☐

The Employee

Minute 4 — Achieve
This week who will you give feedback to?
Completed ☐

Minute 5 — Purpose
How will you connect purpose to pay for an employee or the team this week?
Completed ☐

Minute 6 — Autonomy
How can you support or promote someone's autonomy this week?
Completed ☐

The Job

Minute 7 — Connect
What small thing can you do this week to increase team cohesion?
Completed ☐

Minute 8 — Fun
Where is one place you can inject fun into the job or team this week?
Completed ☐

Minute 9 — Model
What leadership quality will you model this week?
Completed ☐

The Environment

Notes

Made in the USA
Coppell, TX
05 December 2022

87794813R00022